# Indian Stock Market and Investors Strategy -vol 1

## PREFACE

Stock Market is the mitigation of risk through the spreading of investments across multiple entities, which is achieved by the pooling of a number of small investments into a large bucket. Stock Market is the most suitable investment for the common man as it offers an opportunity to invest in a diversified, professionally managed portfolio at a relatively low cost. Enlistment of corporate securities in more than one stock exchange at the same time improves liquidity of securities and functioning of stock exchange there is existence of wild speculation in the Indian stock market Risk is not measurable or quantifiable. But risk is calculated on the basis of historic Volatility Low execution costs make the derivatives especially futures, very suitable for frequent and short *term trading to manage risk more effectively. Investment raises the level of aggregate demand which in turn increases the level of income and employment in the economy. With changes taking place at terrific pace in the field of investments, it has become a specialized activity demanding scientific plans and procedures for success.*

# Acknowledgements

*"It is a long road when you're on your own…"* these lines deeply touch me as I recall the journey of my doctoral research. study in the past years. I am like a soldier who has to fight day and night in order to win the battle. Obviously, no war can be won by a single soldier. I owe a debt of gratitude to them in being patient with my shortcomings and supporting me to develop my skills and knowledge Without the unconditional love of my brother Mr. Puneet Kumar Rawal, my parents Mr. K.V.S Rawal (father)&S.K Rawal (mother), I would not have dared to begin and complete the book. They have always been on my side and backed me to fulfil my desires in anything I choose to pursue. I have got to be grateful to my beloved family members, friends and well-wishers for the constant inspiration, support and prayers they rendered for the completion of this work. Last but not the least, I kneel down in profound humility and deep gratitude before The Lord Almighty for showering his blessings and grace on me through all the stages of this humble endeavor and thereafter.

Dr.Priya Rawal

# INDEX

# CHAPTER – 1

## INTRODUCTION

Market efficiency has an influence on the investment strategy of an investor because if market is efficient, trying to pickup winners will be a waste of time. In an efficient market there will be no undervalued securities offering higher than deserved expected returns, given their risk. On the other hand if markets are not efficient, excess returns can be made by correctly picking the winners. The Random Walk Hypothesis of stock market prices is concerned with the question of whether one can predict future prices from past prices. In its simple form, it states that price changes cannot be predicted from earlier changes in any meaningful manner. Successive price changes in individual securities are independent over time and price changes occur without any significant trends or patterns. Thus past prices contain no useful information as to their future price behavior.

Efficient Market Hypothesis (EMH) states that security prices fully reflect all available information. The weak form of EMH states that the current prices fully reflect the information implied by the past prices, in an efficient market at a given instant of time the prices are assumed to reflect all available information. One would expect the current price of security to be good estimate of its intrinsic values. If the adjustment to new information is instantaneous successive price changes will be independent.

Being a relatively new field in finance, behavioral finance applies psychology to the study of financial behavior. It attempts to study why people buy or sell financial assets based on the psychological principles of decisions making. Instead of completely replacing traditional finance, behavioral finance plays a complementary role in understanding the issues that traditional finance appears to fail to provide satisfactory answers to the questions such as:

(i)     Why do individual investors trade?

(ii)    How do they perform?

(iii)   How do they choose their portfolios?

(iv)    Why do returns vary across stocks for reasons other than risk?

Behavioral finance focuses on how investors interpret and act on information during their investment decision making. The standard assumption underlying traditional finance that investors are always behave in a rational, predictable, and an unbiased manner is relaxed in behavioral finance. Behavioral financial economists have documented plenty of evidence that investors' emotions and cognitive errors are associated with various financial market anomalies. Despite behavioral finance is a relatively new approach in finance research, the topics that behavioral finance covers have grown rapidly in the past decades.

One of the important areas that researchers have

devoted to learn is the role that noise traders play in determining asset prices. The noise trader approach to finance is a vis-à-vis alternative to the efficient markets approach. the noise trader approach to examine whether investor sentiment helps to better describe individual stock returns and can explain the well-documented financial market anomalies. also explores the impacts of investor sentiment on stock volatility and returns at the market level for different countries. Compared to the EMH, the assumptions of the noise trader approach are more plausible as a description of investor behavior and stock markets. They are also the two building blocks of behavioral finance.

The basic assumptions of the noise trader

approach as follows. First, the noise trader approach assumes that some investors are not fully rational and their demand for risky asset is affected by their beliefs or sentiments that are not fully justified by fundamental values. Second, arbitrage defined as trading by fully rational investors not subject to such sentiment is risky and therefore limit.Consequently, the trading behavior of noise traders causes deviations of stock price from fundamental value because changes in investor sentiment are not fully countered by rational investors.

# CHAPTER-2

# MARKET MOVES AND INVESTORS SENTIMENT

The roles of investor sentiment as a conditioning variable and a risk factor in various asset pricing models, respectively, investor sentiment exhibits explanatory power in capturing the financial market anomalies such as the size, value, and momentum effects at the firm level. This book investigates, at the market level, whether investor sentiment affects stock market volatility. Also, examine whether the current monthly investor sentiment measure predicts the market returns for the subsequent month, and whether the market returns are also indirectly influenced by invest sentiment through the risk caused by investor sentiment in the form of volatility.

Traditional financial theories assume that investors are rational and, hence, stock prices should react only to any information related to fundamentals. However, believers who hold the view that stock prices are too volatile to be justified by changes in future dividends. that some investors in the market who trade on 'noise' as if it were profitable information that is associated with fundamentals can affect stock price behaviour. Investors of this kind are called 'noise traders'. Some theoretical model shows that noise traders who have erroneous beliefs can drive stock prices away from fundamental values and increase volatility. empirical studies, provided supportive evidence that investor sentiment or noise trading indeed plays a critical role change in the industrial production index that are capable of predicting monthly stock market returns, instead of using the contemporaneous investor sentiment in the mean equation  the analysis uses the lagged value of investor sentiment.    changes in consumer confidence are positively related to contemporaneous excess stock market returns, sentiment measures are caused by returns.

Using the lagged sentiment rather than the contemporaneous sentiment helps to clearly demonstrate the predictive power of sentiment for the aggregate market returns and avoids the ambiguity of the role that investor sentiment plays in the sentiment return relation. The negative relationship between current consumer confidence level and subsequent excess monthly return is statistically significant not only for the U.S. market but also for France and Italy. The only exception is Japan where the current consumer confidence level boosts the excess market return of next month. In contrast, the lagged value of change in consumer confidence exhibits no predictive power for excess stock market return in most of the countries except for Japan where a positive and statistically significant relation exists. investor sentiment is an important factor in explaining changes in conditional volatility. However, such impact is country-specific. The predictive power of the macroeconomic variables for stock return varies across countries. In general, the lagged values of the dividend yield and the annual measure of inflation often exhibit statistically significant impacts on stock returns across the countries.At the market microstructure level, market making can be a source of market friction that may cause the market irregularity. Some examples are: adverse information between informed traders and market makers, inventory control of market makers and strategic interaction among market participants. Adverse information makes a market maker slowly follow the market regularity because they can only gradually retract information from incoming orders, and thus it lengthens the market irregularity. Inventory control leads to a market maker's intentional irregularity behavior to restore his preferred inventory level.

Strategic interactions can bring various results in terms of the market irregularity. On the other hand, different market microstructures in the stock market can affect this. For instance, two hypotheses can be formed depending on the different impact of the number of market makers. The increased number of market makers may amplify the market irregularity since it increases their aggregate power of controlling prices and absorbing demand/supply shocks than the case of a single market maker. This can be called 'the increased resilience hypotheses. Conversely, multiple market makers for one firm may decrease the size and time length of the irregularity because it increases the informational efficiency of the market due to the higher degree of competition. It can be defined as 'the improved efficiency hypotheses.

Despite the earlier research on theories and some more recent evidence, extensive empirical research on the impact of multiple market makers has not been conducted.  the impact of multiple market makers on price to identify a better supported hypothesis, and also investigates different theories of market making. It adopts intraday return data for empirical analysis. As long as financial markets have existed, people have tried to forecast them, in the hope that good forecasts would bring them great fortunes. In financial practice it is not the question whether it is possible to forecast, but how the future path of a financial time series can be forecasted.

In academia, however, it is merely the question whether series of speculative prices can be forecasted than the question how to forecast. Therefore practice and academics have proceeded along different paths in studying financial time series data. For example, among practitioners fundamental and technical analysis are techniques developed in financial practice according to which guidelines financial time series should and could be forecasted. They are intended to give advice on what and when to buy or sell. In contrast, academics focus on the behavior and characteristics of a financial time series itself and try to explore whether there is certain dependence in successive price changes that could profitably be exploited by various kinds of trading techniques. However, early statistical studies concluded that successive price changes are independent. When empirical findings combined with the efficient markets hypothesis (EMH). According to it , is not possible to exploit any information set to predict future price changes. The evidence in support of the EMH was very extensive, and that contradictory evidence was sparse. Since then the EMH is the central paradigm in financial economics.

An essential difference between chart analysis and fundamental economic analysis is that chartists study only the price action of the market itself, whereas fundamentalists attempt to look for the reasons behind that action. However, both the fundamental analyst and the technical analyst make use of historical data, but in a different manner. The technical analyst claims that all information is gradually discounted in the prices, while the fundamental analyst uses all available information including many other economic variables to compute the 'true' value. The pure technical analyst will never issue a price goal. He only trades on the buy and sell signals his strategies generate. In contrast, the fundamental analyst will issue a price goal that is based on the calculated fundamental value. However in practice investors expect also from technical analysts to issue price goals.

The big advantage of technical analysis over fundamental analysis is that it can be applied fairly easily and cheaply to all kinds of securities prices. Only some practice is needed in recognizing the patterns, but in principle everyone can apply it. Of course, there exist also some complex technical trading techniques, but technical analysis can be made as easy or as difficult as the

user likes. computers make it more easy to come up with sophisticated trading rules, it is better to keep things as simple as possible. Of course fundamental analysis can also be made as simple as one likes. For example look at the number of cars parked at the lot of the shopping mall to get an indication of consumers' confidence in the national economy.

Usually more (macro) economic variables are needed. That makes fundamental analysis more costly than technical analysis. An advantage of technical analysis from an academic point of view is that it is much easier to test the forecasting power of well defined objective technical trading rules than to test the forecasting power of trading rules based on fundamentals. For testing technical trading rules only data is needed on prices, volumes and dividends, which can be obtained fairly easily. However in practice investors expect also from technical analysts to issue price goals.

Neither fundamental nor technical analysis will lead to sure profits. Furthermore, fundamental analysts do not always report what they think, as became publicly known sometime the "Long Term Capital Management" (LTCM) fund filed for bankruptcy. This hedge fund was trading on the basis of mathematical models. Under leadership of the New York Federal Reserve Bank, one the twelve central banks in the US, the financial world had to raise a great amount of money to prevent a big catastrophe. Because LTCM had large obligations in the derivatives markets, which they could not fulfill anymore, default of payments would have an impression on the profits of the financial companies who had taken the counterpart positions in the market. A sudden bankruptcy of LTCM could have led to a chain reaction on Wall Street and the rest of the financial world.

Despite the fact that chartists have a strong belief in their forecasting abilities, in academia it remains questionable whether technical trading based on patterns or trends in past prices has any statistically significant forecasting power and whether it can profitably be exploited after correcting for transaction costs and risk. by analyzing the weekly forecasting results of well-known professional agencies, such as Financial services and fire insurance companies, The ability of selecting a specific stock which should generate superior returns, as well as the ability of forecasting the movement of the stock market itself is studied. Thousands of predictions are recorded finds no statistically signficant forecasting performance. Wall Street Journal which presented forecasts for the stock market based on the Dow Theory. Again no evidence of forecasting power is found. However, although the number of months the stock market declined exceeded the number of months the stock market rose, the fact that readers prefer good news to bad, and that a forecaster who presents a cheerful point of view thereby attracts more followers without whom he would probably be unable to remain long in the forecasting business.

According to the random walk hypothesis trends in prices are spurious and purely accidentally manifestations. Therefore, trading systems based on past information should not generate profits in excess of equilibrium expected profits or returns.

It became commonly accepted that the study of past price trends and patterns is no more useful in predicting future price movements than throwing a dart at the list of stocks in a daily newspaper. However the dependence in price changes can be of such a complicated form that standard linear statistical tools, such as serial correlations, may provide misleading measures of the degree of dependence in the data.

# CHAPTER-3

# FUNDAMENTAL ANALYSIS

The purpose of fundamental securities analysis is to find and explore all economic variables that influence the future earnings of a financial asset.

These fundamental variables measure different economic circumstances, ranging from macro-economic (inflation, interest rates, oil prices, recessions, unemployment, etc.),industry specific (competition, demand/supply, technological changes, etc.) and firm specific (company growth, dividends, earnings, lawsuits, strikes etc.) circumstances. On the basis of these 'economic fundamentals' a fundamental analyst tries to compute the true underlying value, also called the fundamental value, of a financial asset. According to the firm-foundation theory the fundamental value of an asset should be equal to the discounted value of all future cash flows the asset will generate. The discount factor is taken to be the interest rate plus a risk premium and therefore the fundamental analyst must also make expectations about future interest rate developments. The fundamental value is thus based on historical data and expectations about future developments extracted from them.

Only 'news', which is new facts about the economic variables determining the true value of the fundamental asset, can change the fundamental value. If the computed fundamental value is higher (lower) than the market price, then the fundamental analyst concludes that the market over- (under-) values the asset. A long (short) position in the market should be taken to profit from this supposedly under- (over-) valuation. The philosophy behind fundamental analysis is that in the end, when enough traders realize that the market is not correctly pricing the asset, the market mechanism of demand/supply, will force the price of the asset to converge to its fundamental value.

It is assumed that fundamental analysts who have better access to information and who have a more sophisticated system in interpreting and weighing the influence of information on future earnings will earn more than analysts who have less access to information and have a less sophisticated system in interpreting and weighing information. It is emphasized that sound investment principles will produce sound investment results, eliminating the psychology of the investors. What's needed is a sound intellectual framework for making decisions and the ability to keep emotions from corroding that framework. The sillier the market's behavior, the greater the opportunity for the business-like investor." However, it is questionable whether traders can perform a complete fundamental analysis in determining the true value of a financial asset. An important critique is that fundamental traders have to examine a lot of different economic variables and that they have to know the precise effects of all these variables on the future cash flows of the asset. Furthermore, it may happen that the price of an asset, for example due to overreaction by traders, persistently deviates from the fundamental value. In that case, short term fundamental trading cannot be profitable and therefore it is said that fundamental analysis should be used to make long-term predictions. Then a problem may be that a fundamental trader does not have enough wealth and/or enough patience to wait until convergence finally occurs.

Furthermore, it could be that financial markets affect fundamentals, which they are supposed to reflect. In that case they do not merely discount the future, but they help to shape it and financial markets will never tend toward equilibrium. Thus it is clear that it is a most hazardous task to perform accurate fundamental analysis. On the other hand it may be possible for a trader to make a fortune by free riding on the expectations of all other traders together. Through the market mechanism of demand and supply the expectations of those traders will eventually be reflected in the asset price in a more or less gradual way. If a trader is engaged in this line of thinking, to leaves fundamental analysis and to moves into the area of technical analysis.

# CHAPTER-4

# TECHNICAL ANALYSIS

Technical analysis is the study of past price movements with the goal to predict future Price movements from the past. A high proportion of chief dealers view technical and fundamental analysis as complementary forms of analysis and a substantial proportion suggest that technical advice may be self-fulfilling. There is a feeling among market participants that it is important to have a notion of Chartism, because many traders use it, and may therefore influence market prices.

It is said that Chartism can be used to exploit

marke movements generated by less sophisticated, 'noise traders'. The general consensus among technical analysts is that there is no need to look at the fundamentals, because everything that is happening in the world can be seen in the price charts. A popular saying among chartists is that "a picture is worth a ten thousand words." "If the market makes numbers out of information, one should be able to reverse the process and get information out of numbers."

The philosophy behind technical analysis is that information is gradually discounted in the price of an asset. Except for a crash once in a while there is no 'big bang' price movement that immediately discounts all available information. It is said that price gradually moves to new highs or new lows and that trading volume goes with the prevailing trend. Therefore most popular technical trading rules are trend following techniques such as moving averages and filters.

Technical analysis tries to detect changes in investors' sentiments in an early stage and tries to profit from them. It is said that these changes in sentiments cause certain patterns to occur repeatedly in the price charts, because people react the same in equal circumstances. A lot of 'subjective' pattern recognition techniques are therefore described in the technical analysis literature which have fancy names, such as head & shoulders, double top, double bottoms, triangles, rectangles, etc., which should be traded on after their pattern is completed. Most popular technical trading rules are based on moving averages.

A moving average is a recursively updated, for example daily, weekly or monthly, average of past prices. A moving average smoothes out erratic price movements and is supposed to reflect the underlying trend in prices. A buy (sell) signal is said to be generated at time t if the price crosses the moving average upwards (downwards) at time Furthermore, in financial practice technical analysis is criticized because of its highly subjective nature. It is said that there are probably as many methods of combining and interpreting the various techniques as there are chartists themselves.

Despite the fact that chartists have a strong belief in their forecasting abilities, in academia it remains questionable whether technical trading based on patterns or trends in past prices has any statistically significant forecasting power and whether it can profitably be exploited after correcting for transaction costs and risk.

## CHAPTER-5

## FUNDAMENTAL ANALYSIS VERSUS TECHNICAL ANALYSIS

The big advantage of technical analysis over fundamental analysis is that it can be applied fairly easily and cheaply to all kinds of securities prices. Only some practice is needed in recognizing the patterns, but in principle everyone can apply it. Of course, there exist also some complex technical trading techniques, but technical analysis can be made as easy or as difficult as the user likes.

Of course fundamental analysis can also be made as simple as one likes. For example, look at the number of cars parked at the lot of the shopping mall to get an indication of consumers' confidence in the national economy. Usually more (macro) economic variables are needed. That makes fundamental analysis more costly than technical analysis. An advantage of technical analysis from an academic point of view is that it is much easier to test the forecasting power of well-defined objective technical trading rules than to test the forecasting power of trading rules based on fundamentals.

For testing technical trading rules only data is needed on prices, volumes and dividends, which can be obtained fairly easily. An essential difference between chart analysis and fundamental economic analysis is that chartists study only the price action of the market itself, whereas fundamentalists attempt to look for the reasons behind that action. However, both the fundamental analyst and the technical analyst make use of historical data, but in a different manner.

The technical analyst claims that all information is gradually discounted in the prices, while the fundamental analyst uses all available information including many other economic variables to compute the 'true' value. The pure technical analyst will never issue a price goal. He only trades on the buy and sell signals his strategies generate. In contrast, the fundamental analyst will issue a price goal that is based on the calculated fundamental value.

However in practice investors expect also from technical analysts to issue price goals. There are three principles underlying technical analysis. The first is that all information is gradually discounted in the prices. Through the market mechanism the expectations, hopes, dreams and believes of all investors are reflected in the prices.

A technical analyst argues that the best adviser

you can get is the market itself and there is no need to explore fundamental information. Second, technical analysis assumes that prices move in upward, downward or sideways trends. Therefore most technical trading techniques are trend-following instruments. The third assumption is that history repeats itself. Under equal conditions investors will react the same leading to price patterns which can be recognized in the data. Technical analysts claim that if a pattern is detected in an early stage, profitable trades can be made. Besides testing the random walk theory with serial correlation tests, runs tests and by applying technical trading rules used in practice, academics were searching for a theory that could explain the random walk behavior of stock prices.

properly anticipated prices fluctuate randomly ."that in an informational efficient market price changes must be unforecastable if they are properly anticipated, i.e., if they fully incorporate the expectations and information of all market participants. Because news is announced randomly, since otherwise it would not be news anymore, prices must fluctuate randomly. This important observation, combined with the notion that positive earnings are the reward for bearing risk, and the earlier empirical findings that successive price changes are independent, led to the efficient markets hypothesis. Especially the notion of trade-off between reward and risk distinguishes the efficient markets hypothesis from the random walk theory, which is merely a purely statistical model of returns.

A financial market is called weak efficient, if no trading rule can be developed that can forecast future price movements on the basis of past prices. Secondly, a financial market is called semi-strong efficient, if it is impossible to forecast future price movements on the basis of publicly known information. Finally, a financial market is called strong efficient if on the basis of all available information, also inside information, it is not possible to forecast future price movements. Semi-strong efficiency implies weak form efficiency.

Strong efficiency implies semi-strong and weak efficiency. If the weak form of the EMH can be rejected, then also the semi strong and strong form of the EMH can be rejected.

The efficient markets model is very extensive, and that contradictory evidence is sparse. The impact of the empirical findings on random walk behavior and the conclusion in academia that financial asset prices are and should be unforecastable was so large, that it took a while before new academic literature on technical trading was published. Financial analysts heavily debated the efficient markets hypothesis. However, as argued by academics, even if the theory of Samuelson would be wrong, then there are still many empirical findings of no forecast ability. Market technicians kept arguing that statistical tests of any kind are less capable of detecting subtle patterns in stock price data than the human eye.

# CHAPTER-6

## TRADING RANGE BREAK-OUT

Trading rules consists of trading range break-out (TRB) strategies, also called support-and-resistance strategies. The TRB strategy uses support and resistance levels. If during a certain period of time the price does not fall below (rise beyond) a certain price level, this price level is called a support (resistance) level. According to technical analysts, there is a "battle between buyers and sellers" at these price levels. The market buys at the support level after a price decline and sells at the resistance level after a price rise. If the price breaks through the support (resistance) level, an important technical trading signal is generated. The sellers (buyers) have won the "battle". At the support (resistance) level the market has become a net seller (buyer). This indicates that the market will move to a subsequent lower (higher) level. The support (resistance) level will change into a resistance (support) level. To implement the TRB strategy, support-and-resistance levels are defined as local minima and maxima of the closing prices. If the price falls (rises) through the local minimum (maximum) a sell (buy) signal is generated and a short (long) position is taken in the market. If the price moves between the local minimum and maximum the position in the market is maintained until there is a new breakthrough. The TRB strategy will also be extended with a %-band filter, a time delay filter, a fixed holding period and a stop-loss. Real-time traders live from moment to moment.Such is the pull of a live data feed, it's often a challenge to see the big picture. But this you must do if you want to survive and prosper.Visualizing the current trade as one of a series helps to maintain your discipline and lower your emotional cholesterol. But there's one trading tool that will really improve your performance more than anything else. A trader's diary. Don't be scared off by the sentimental connotations of keeping a diary. "Dear Diary... today I... " this is not. Your own trading diary can be computer-based - via a word-processing document or a simple text file saved to your desktop. Or you may find a traditional pen and paper version more effective. (There is something about writing on paper that makes it more personal. Probably the way the hand and eye coordinate with the brain. Plus you've probably got enough applications running when you're trading in real-time!) Another option is to a personal tape recorder. Good if you prefer speaking to writing. Whatever format you use... what will you actually write (or say)? Anything. Don't worry about grammar. Make one-word notes of what's happening. Sure, you can note down the facts and figures - stock code, time and date, position size, entry price, stop loss, exit price. But also - and more importantly - record your thoughts. If you were hesitant about getting in the trade, say so. If you're terrified now you're in (the dreaded"Trader's Remorse") then make a note of it. When you exit, say why. Stopped out? Took profits? Why? How did you feel before the exit? How do you feel now, afterwards?This only takes a few seconds to record this ongoing commentary of your own trading. But the information you get can be priceless. Here's why: At the end of each week, preferably at the weekend when the markets are closed, review the week's entries. You can guarantee that you'll see a pattern in your behavior. There is probably something you are doing consistently that's causing negative results. And once you've identified the problem, the solution usually becomes obvious. Do this exercise every week, and also every month to get a longer term perspective. Only you can do this for yourself. Nobody looks after your own affairs better than you do. You don't need the latest million dollar trading system to be successful in this business.Look within. You may be amazed with the results.

## CHAPTER-7

## CONCLUSION

Investor sentiment affects stock market returns and volatility, and also explores how fundamental values help to forecast stock returns. In addition, it also examines whether a sentiment measure that primarily reflects the perceptions of the producers about the prospect of economy predicts stock price behavior at the market level, different approaches which are used for research and hypothesis which are test for research work and formulation of base hypothesis. The movement of stock prices is highly sensitive to changes in fundamentals of the economy and to the changes in expectations about future prospects. If the economy grows rapidly, the industry is also expected to show rapid growth reflecting the prosperous outlook for its sales and earnings which would result in increased cash flows' and stock prices. On consolidating these two general views exist among the investors and practitioners with regard to such relationship. The first relationship views that the changes in stock market cause fluctuations in macroeconomic environment of a country and the second perceives that the stock market development and changes are the rash of economic conditions of the country. In other words the former case implies that stock market leads economic activity, whereas the latter suggests that it lags economic activity and which is more important for a security analyst. According to one interpretation of the efficient-market hypothesis (EMH), only changes in fundamental factors, such as the outlook for margins, profits or dividends, ought to affect share prices beyond the short term, where random 'noise' in the system may prevail. (But this largely theoretic academic viewpoint known as 'hard' EMH also predicts that little or no trading should take place, contrary to fact, since prices are already at or near equilibrium, having priced in all public knowledge.)The 'hard' efficient-market hypothesis is sorely tested and does not explain the cause of events. Such as the crash in 1987, when the Dow Jones Industrial Average plummeted 22.6 percent---the largest-ever one-day fall in the United States. Investors in stock market are interested primarily in selling securities for more than they paid for it, including the receipt of dividend during the period security is held The investors hope to achieve a higher reward than they would have been by placing the amount of money in a bank deposit or a bond investment. Stock prices are determined by a host of factors ranging from rational and fundamental factors to irrational psychosomatic factors. In Nutshell It's Concluded That If Prices Are Based On Investor Expectations, Then Knowing What A Security Should Sell For (Fundamental Analysis) Becomes Less Important Than Knowing What Other Investors Expect It To Sell For. That's Not To Say That Knowing What A Security Should Sell For Isn't Important It Is. But There Is Usually A Fairly Strong Consensus Of A Stock's Future Earnings That The Average Investor Cannot Disprove. For identifying the research gap empirical findings of considerable number of research on various dimensions of stock market investments and its price behavior in various markets across the globe at different points of time, concluded that in such inefficient market, equity research will produce better results as there will be frequent mismatch between price and value that provides opportunities to the long-term value oriented investor. More precisely the price or intrinsic value of a common stock shall be determined on the basis of certain basic economic factors or economic fundamentals. This is because the real value of a stock is always equal to the discounted value of its future cash flows in the form of earnings and dividend. These cash flows vary along with the changes in macroeconomic performance of the country, the state of the industry and also with the specific performance of the firms issuing shares. So the fundamental analysis covers a detailed examination of the underlying forces which affect the wellbeing of the economy, industry group and companies. Technical analysts (followers of technical analysis) do not consider any of the company's fundamentals for their stock selection. Technical analysts test historical data to establish specific rules for buying and selling securities with the objective of maximizing profit and minimizing risk of loss. In other words, technical approach is concerned primarily with price action and trying to identify patterns that repeat themselves. For identifying the past trend in share price data, the technical analysts mainly use certain charts and chart patterns, hence the technical analysts are also known as chartists. In addition to past price data, technical analysis also considers other statistics such as volume of trading and stock market indices mainly for capturing the general trend prevailing in the market. Technically based trading systems also can provide more objective buy/sell decisions, as long as the trader or researcher avoids interjecting his own subjective analysis into his computer output. In predicting the stock market movement, two theories have had significant impact on market research Efficient market hypothesis (EMH) and Random walk theory. Technical analysis will not be able to consistently produce excess returns, though some forms of fundamental analysis may still provide excess returns.

www.ingramcontent.com/pod-product-compliance
Lightning Source LLC
Chambersburg PA
CBHW080607180526
45168CB00007B/2820